Sales:

Foolproof Method to CRUSH Your Numbers - Selling, Sales Techniques, and Sales Strategy

Table of Contents

*Foolproof Method to CRUSH Your Numbers
- Selling, Sales Techniques, and Sales
Strategy*

After the buying	20
When they plan to use it	20
After using it	21
Much later	21
60 -70% customers	22
During the buying process	23
After the buying	24
When they plan to use it	24
After using it	25
Much later	25
40- 50% customers	26
During the buying process	26
After the buying	27
When they plan to use it	28
After using it	28
Much later	29
20 – 30% customers	29
During the buying process	30
After the buying	31
When they plan to use it	32
While using it	32
Much later	33

Foolproof Method to CRUSH Your Numbers
- Selling, Sales Techniques, and Sales
Strategy

*Foolproof Method to CRUSH Your Numbers
- Selling, Sales Techniques, and Sales
Strategy*

distribute, sell, use, quote or paraphrase any part or the content within this book without the consent of the author or copyright owner. Legal action will be pursued if this is breached.

Disclaimer Notice:

Please note the information contained within this document is for educational and entertainment purposes only. Every attempt has been made to provide accurate, up to date and reliable complete information. No warranties of any kind are expressed or implied. Readers acknowledge that the author is not engaging in the rendering of legal, financial, medical or professional advice.

Introduction

For any business, small or big, "sales" is the most important aspect to consider. Whether it is the sale of commercial products or services, it is important for the business to focus on selling as much of these to as many customers as possible.

But oftentimes, companies do not pay attention to their sales strategies and end up having mediocre numbers. Despite having amazing products and services on offer, they will not have the right sales techniques and strategies to supplement them, and thus, end up having reduced sales.

This, however, can be effectively dealt with, to improve the overall sales of a company and help acquire a bigger and stronger customer base. This book contains proven steps and strategies to help you increase your sales techniques and tactics, and crush your sales numbers. There is also a bonus chapter on why it is important for you to have a good sales strategy in place.

Foolproof Method to CRUSH Your Numbers - Selling, Sales Techniques, and Sales Strategy

I want to thank you for choosing this book and hope you find the content informative and it helps you in improving your sales strategies.

Chapter 1: Importance Of Employing Sales Techniques

In this first chapter of the book, we will look at why it is important for you to employ sales techniques and how it impacts your business.

Before we delve into the advantages, let us first understand the differences between sales strategies and sales techniques. Strategies are broader, long-term plans that are meant for the overall good of the business. They will take into account all the resources that are at the company's disposal.

Sales techniques on the other hand, are short term; flexible plans that are employed by companies and consider only a few resources that are needed to attain the desirable outputs. A company needs to make use of both in order to increase their sales.

Higher sales

For any business, a higher sales rate is always a major goal. The main advantage of using sales strategies and technique is to help increase the number of sales in a month. With a plan in place, it will be easy for you to improve on sales numbers, as you will have a chance to sell your product to more and more people. Most companies employ sales strategies and techniques to increase their sales for products and services that are both in season and out of season. They will see an improvement in the number of sales within a couple of months of employing these strategies. However, it is important to not expect too much from it at one go and you need to have reasonable expectations.

Meeting monthly goals

By making use of sales strategies and techniques, you can meet your monthly sales goals. It will be easy for you to attain the sales numbers that you have set out to achieve in a month. For this, you will have to sketch out a proper plan and work according to it, in order to meet your goals. Say for example you wish to sell 500 necklaces this month. With a strategy and a technique in place, you will have a chance to meet that number and can probably surpass it with ease.

Faster sales

When it comes to the life of a business, you never know how long or short it will last. So for this reason, you must try and have as many sales as possible within a short period of time. This is possible if you have a sales strategy, or technique, in place. You will realize that your sales are now going at a faster pace and that you are able to sell more in a month than you previously did. So it is always better to have a sales strategy in place if you wish to experience a faster sales growth.

Lesser costs

When you have a working sales strategy in place, you will realize that your overall costs are reducing. It will be easier for you to plan out your budget, as you will know exactly where and how your resources need to be utilized. With reduced costs, you will have a chance to provide better service; which will ultimately benefit you, as your customers will be happy. You will have to spend less on your labor, marketing and all other major expenses and it will work out to your advantage. It makes sense to employ a technique that will help you save on money. So adopting these sales strategies is a great idea for you and you can save on a lot of money with them.

Better products

With a good strategy in place, you can improve your product by understanding your market and target audience. You can conduct surveys to find what your audience wants and supply them with appropriate products. Your products can improve both your customer base and your reputation and this will, in turn, boost your sales. So a strategy is extremely important when it comes to improving your company on an overall basis and you can use the surplus money to invest into R&D for your products.

Business expansion

Once your company's sales start to grow, you will have to pander to more and more customers. For this, you need to expand your business in order to meet the heightened level of demand for your products. Business expansion is one of the main advantages of having a good sales strategy, as it will enable you to make more money, which you can utilize for your expansion plans. Say for example: you own a travel agency that deals in train and air bookings. Through your unique marketing strategies you are able to sell a lot of tickets. Once people get to hear about your great service, you will have to expand your business and try an incorporate bus and car bookings as well. This will help you satisfy a larger customer base.

Satisfying customers

It is obvious that your customer base will expand when you have a good sales strategy in place. Adding to it will be your current customers, who will also continue to buy your products and services, owing to your growth in popularity. So you will have a chance to hold on to your current customers and also have newer ones come in, just by making use of the best sales strategies and techniques that are fit for your business.

Competitive advantage

The main aim of sales strategies is to give you and your products an edge over your competitors and their products. You will have a chance to surpass them and your products and services will gain more popularity if you choose the right strategies. For this, you will have to employ the best, in order to be the best. You will only get mediocre results if you employ mediocre strategies and thus, have to come up with sales techniques that will help you crush your sales numbers along with your competitors

Market share

Increasing market share is a matter of pride for any company. Imagine starting out by having just a 1 or 2% presence and growing to 20 or 30% in a matter of a few years, it will put you on the map and how. But for this to be possible, you will have to employ all the best strategies and techniques to increase your sales and attain Earth shattering numbers. This may sound like a daunting task, but can be made possible, if you have the right approach and resources to supplement your vision.

Chapter 2: The 80/ 20 Analysis

In the previous chapter, we looked at the importance of having sound sales strategies and techniques in place, in order to attain heightened sales. In this one, we will look at one of the most preferred sales strategies that are adopted to help boost monthly sales.

This strategy is known as the 80/20 analysis and is explained as under.

What is it?
The 80/20 analysis is a technique that is used to interpret sales and profit ratios. It is a statistical analysis that is carried out to understand what percentages of customers influence the sales and what percentage of products bring in the most sales. In simpler terms, it is used to understand what type of customers will bring in sales and which products will do the same for a company.

The two values that are considered are 80 and 20, which together form 100. Here, the 80 will always form your outcome or your output and the 20 is your input or effort.

That is, 80% will be the final sales output and 20% will be your effort. Let us assume that you are calculating your sales output in regard to the number of customers that bring in business. You will have 80% sales thanks to just 20% of your customers. The remaining 80% customers will bring in just 20% business. Similarly, 80% of your profits come courtesy of 20% products and services and the rest 80% will bring in just 20% profit.

How to apply it

To make use of this technique, you must first narrow down your statistics. Start by going through all your records and noting down all the important ones. This should include your sales per customer, how much business particular categories of customers have brought in, your product and service sales, different types of sales avenues viz. web sales, store sales, catalogue sales etc. These are just standard things that companies consider and you can account for any other sales related data that is deemed important.

Once you make a note of all these, you must arrange them in an order of your choice. Generally, the most important ones are mentioned first and the rest in descending order.

Once done, you must write down their values next to their names. Say for example: you are considering web sales; write down the number of sales that have taken place in that particular month.

Then, next to the particular values, write down the total values. That is, next to the web sales amount, you must write down the total sale value that has come from all avenues. Similarly, if you wish to calculate your catalogue sale customers, then write down how many have ordered from your catalogue and write down the total number of customers next to it.

Now convert all your numbers into percentages by making use of the specific value and the total value. For example: if your web sales figure is 300 and total sales are 1000, then it will be 30%. Similarly, convert each of your data into percentage form.

Once done, arrange them in descending order for easy reading and write down the cumulative percentages. You must stop when the percentage reaches 100%. So let's say you have 23% in the first column and 12% in the next then the cumulative % will be 35%. If the next percentage will be 17% then the cumulative will be 52%. Similarly, go on calculating until you reach 100%.

Now you can start reading your percentages to understand which bunch of customers are bringing in most sales and which products are selling the best.

In the web sales example we arrived at 30%. So 30% of your profit is coming via web sales. Similarly, you must find out for all your customer categories and products. However, remember that it need not always be exact 80/20 figures and can also be 83/21, 80/25 etc. Here, you must interpret it as 21% of customers brining in 83% sales and 25% products brining in 80% profit etc.

After you find the number of customers that are bringing in the most sales, and the products or services that are selling the most, you can start to promote them better and retain a majority of your business giving customers.

Benefits of the analysis

There are many advantages to using this method and some are as follows.

- The very first advantage is that, you get a chance to identify your most important customers and have a fair chance at retaining them, by catering to them in a better way

- Using this analysis will help you identify your key products and services and can focus on improving them

- It will also give away information on why the particular group of customers is keen on buying the particular product or service

- You will get a chance to cut down on the products that are not working well and can also cut down on those customers, who are not bringing in much business

Chapter 3: Sales Strategies And Techniques To Crush Numbers

In the previous chapter, we looked at the 80/20 analysis and saw how it can be used to improve your sales.

In this chapter, we will read on the sales strategies and techniques that you can employ in order to increase your sales.

Research

The very first strategy to employ is market research. Each and every product has a particular market for it. You need to identify and understand your market in order to sell you products better. Let us look at things you need to do in order to conduct research.

Survey

A survey is a technique used to understand who your customers are and what it is that they want. You can also conduct a survey on your product and ask people what they think of it. You need to conduct a research on the market areas where your products will sell best. For this, you can send out researchers with some forms and get them to ask people for their opinion. These response sheets will give you a good idea of what people are looking for, and how they rate your products. Once you have an idea of everything, you can move to the next step.

Audience base

For any business, it is important to identify the audience base and segregate it. This means that you identify the entire gamut and then classify them according to their common links. Say for example you classify your audience based on their age or gender or class. It will depend on what your company sells. If you have a lot of products on offer then you must consider all the different groups, but if you have only a few specific things like charm bracelets, then your audience will be youngsters. You must have a clear idea of who your audience is, in order to improve your sales.

Customer wants

It is always vital to consider the customer's wants. Say for example: you deal in bracelets, you will have to understand whether they like the designs that you put out and if they would like some changes in it. Generally, most people in the same category will think alike and one or two opinions can be generalized. You must, however, keep with the times and change your designs as per the season and depending on what your audience likes and dislikes.

Customer evaluation

For any sales person, it is important to make a sales pitch depending on what the customer is looking for. Here are the things to consider when you catering to a particular kind of audience.

Identify the main person

When you look at a group of people that are shopping, you must identify the main person amongst them. The main person need not always be the one with the money. It can also be someone who makes all the decisions for the family. In order to close the deal, the person must successfully identify the main person in the group and speak with them about any of the offers that you wish to promote. You must approach them personally, but if you end up appealing to the wrong person, then you might not be able to effectively sell your product or service to them.

Create urgency

Once you understand who the main shopper is, you must take steps to create urgency. The person must be motivated to not waste any more time and buy the product immediately. The best trick for this is to say that an offer is about to end or that the stocks don't last long. This will prompt them to buy the product immediately. You will be able to close the sale if you use this trick on the right type of customer.

Assist

Remember to always assist your customers. Although some will like to do the research themselves, not all will take fancy to reading the labels. If you personally assist them in your store by helping them pick out things and give them useful information on the product, then you are most likely going to sell the product to them. For this, you have to be present in the moment and look at people who want assistance. You can also volunteer to hold their bag if you like as it will help them better concentrate on shopping.

Psychology

When it comes to selling products, marketing plays a big part. You have to make use of certain marketing tricks to get your customers to buy your products. Here are some of the tricks explained.

Pricing

When you price your products make sure that it ends in decimals. This always has an impact on the buyer, as they will feel good about getting save the .1. So your price tags should always read 92.99$ or 39.99$ etc. as this will be much better than pricing it at 93$ and 40$. The customer will anyway round it off himself or herself but it will appeal better to them when they look at the prices in decimals.

Offers

All customers love to buy products that have offers running. Some offers such as buy 2 get 50% off or buy 2 air tickets and get a business class upgrade for free etc. are all examples of offers. These offers will give the customer more of the same product, as opposed to different products. The customer will be happy to walk away with more quantity by paying the same price, or only a little extra.

Free gifts

Most customers love getting free gifts. They will be thrilled if you give away something complimentary with a product that they bought. Say for example they bought a washing machine, if you give away 5 packs of quality detergent that will help them wash their clothes, then it will make them very happy. Giving complimentary gifts always does its trick, and you can decide on something that will make them happy.

Customer retention

Retention refers to converting potential buyers into sure shot buyers. Remember that it is always easier to retain current customers than to look for new ones. For this, you need to understand the different categories of customers. You need to influence each to retain them for many years. These categories are broad classifications and you must understand who falls into what category to influence them the right way. You will have to quickly assess the person and categorize him or her without wasting too much time. This is crucial as 1 old customer is equal to 10 new ones and so; it is best to hold on to what you have.

80-90% customers

These people are extremely organized and will have quite the sum at their disposal. They will be logical and cannot be fooled easily. They will prefer to shop once a month and buy everything that they need. They will have a set plan to follow and buy the products accordingly. In order to retain these customers you must offer them products that will appeal to them and will go well with whatever that they have bought. It is always best to run up to them as soon as they buy a product and tell them about how what you chose, will go well with it. They will thank you for your suggestions and might take at least 60% of whatever you suggest. Make sure you choose quality products, as they are sure to return once they feel satisfied with what they bought.

These are logical and will reason it out with you. So you have to be prepared to answer all their doubts and get them to buy your products. They will be fully equipped with a shopping list and make their way to the shopping center knowing exactly what they will leave with. The trick is to not lay any traps for them at all as they will quickly surmise it and prefer to not shop with you. So you don't want to run that risk with them and must do whatever you can to not fool them with anything. As we saw in the 80/20 analysis, 20% of your customers will bring you your 80% business and so, it is safe to assume that this 20% will be your 80%-90% customers and so, it is best to keep them as satisfied as possible.

Retention techniques

During the buying process

This is the most important time to influence these buyers and get them to say yes to you. They will be extremely logical and say yes to you if they think you are making them a good offer. Say for example they are there to buy a toaster. If along with that you also offer them a juicer then they will be highly interested in it. This is because they will want something to make their breakfast process easy and by offering them the juicer, you will be contributing positively towards it. They will be happy with your suggestion and their confidence in you will grow. Similarly, have a slew of offers ready for them in keeping with whatever they have bought already. You can also have a demonstration readied and show them what you have on offer for them. It will be easier for you to close the deal if you do so.

After the buying

After they successfully buy whatever you offer to them, they will be interested in the next product you have. But there needs to be a limit. You cannot keep offering them things in loop. There should come a point when you stop and they are fully satisfied with your service. If you make it a never ending loop then they will feel offended and you will end up upsetting your valued repeat customers. So have a number in mind and show them only those many products. Generally, stopping at 3 is ideal and make sure no two are closely related with each other.

When they plan to use it

When they are using it, you must call in from time to time and offer suggestions and demonstrations to them. They will be happy to get it from you. You must know exactly when to call them to advise them. This you can do by studying their history and understanding when they use something. You can also offer to send personal over to help set it up for them and get them to like all the services that you have on offer for them. If you do this, then you are sure to keep your important repeat customers happy and get them back to your store quite often.

After using it

After a few days when they would have used the product for some time, you must again call to know the status of the product. You must also suggest an upgrade of the product and tell them about its unique features. These features should be appealing and much better than what the product already has. You have to sell it to them intelligently and get them to like whatever you are selling them. Once they are sold on it, you can either offer to send over the upgraded product or convince them to come over by telling them they are a lot more upgraded varieties available at your store.

Much later

These are your repeat customers and those that will walk into your store for life, provided you keep them happy. So the best thing to do is to keep calling them regularly and sending them consistent offers. If by any chance you have lost touch with them, then it is fine to contact them again as they will still be obliging and easy to take wherever out offer to them. They will be interested in taking what you give them. So get them on call not matter how long it's been and give them a good offer that they simply cannot refuse.

60 -70% customers

This is a range of customers, which is smart and logical, but not as much as the previous ones. They might not be as organized and will prefer to roam around listlessly. But they will end up buying everything that they want and to influence them, you can try running up to them at the last moment with your suggestions. They are most likely to buy the products if you create urgency, as they will think of it as a good chance to buy these instead of having more trips.

These customers can be qui emotional and will be picky about their brands. They will choose only those that they have been using for a long time and will not look at others. However, if you put on your best selling hat, then you have with chance to influence them and consider another product that you are offering to them. They will hesitate a little as they would have made their choice but if you effectively tell them why your choice is better than theirs then they will settle for it. These are the type of people who will get confused even if there is just a small variation in the price of the product. So don't offer them things that of different price ranges and show only those that are within their set budget.

During the buying process

These people are way trickier as compared to the Raipur type and it will be difficult for you to sell something extra to them. They will have a pre-determined mindset to buy certain things and they will not be interested in your suggestions, especially if they are last minute. So don't show them something when they are in line to hill what they have. You will end up upsetting them. So give them ample time to think about the product you are offering to them and they will not disappoint you. In fact, they will start trusting you and understand that you are doing your best to help them out and lessen their efforts.

After the buying

Once they buy what you have offered and understood your true intentions, they will be happy to spread word about your store. In fact, they will be keen on coming back and taking suggestions from you. So it will become progressively easier for you with these customers and you might end up making them your 80-90% customers. But for that, you have to put in consistent efforts and not lose you enthusiasm. Make a straightforward offer to them and they will happily take it. Don't have any intention of fooling them, as they will be quick to catch you. So keep it simple and effective.

When they plan to use it

Just as was with the previous category, it is a good time to offer them combinations and other products that will go with whatever they already have. They will take your offer and be glad. So call them when they are using it and tell them you have a complimentary product that will make it worthwhile for them. You can get them to visit you again and tell them about other products. You will have a great opportunity to influence them and get them to buy bigger and better things from you.

After using it

After they have used the products and you have won their confidence, you can sell a lot of things to them without worrying too much. You would have converted most of them into your repeat customers and they will be glad to take your suggestions and opinions. You can offer the, products that come with freebies and retain the interest. Trust building is vital for any type of customer and you have to do your best to win over their confidence and get them to like whatever you plan to give to them.

Much later

As was mentioned earlier, they tend to get emotionally attached to things. This can be brands, products or stores. So once you successfully establish an emotional connect with them, they will come back to you and buy from you again. To further enhance the relationship, you can send them personal cards; special invites and other such things that will make them feel special. They will definitely come back to you and might also get others along, which will be extremely beneficial to you. You have to make them understand that you will always be there for them and not disappoint them in any regard.

40- 50% customers

This category is a lot like the previous in that, they will be disorganized and listless. It will be tough to use urgency as a means to influence these, as they will not be motivated to buy it. These customers will be slightly restless but will love to go through every possible aisle and pick up everything that there is to. To appeal to these customers, you must have something fancy and eye catching arranged in such a way that it appeals to them to pick it up. It is ideal to place these things at the last aisle, as they will be tempted to pick up everything that catches their fancy and will immediately bill it.

These customers are tough to please and will have a pre determined mind set about certain things. It will not be easy to fool them and they will have a logical mindset.

During the buying process

These customers are very easy to influence when they are about to buy something. You will have it quite easy with them if you offer them combo offers or something similar.

26

They will not refuse what you offer them and will be pleased with their purchase. Just as they walk around the store, you must keep an eye on them. When they pick up something, simply run to them with a similar product but having a special offer. Once you build that trust, they will be glad to take your advice. So try offering more than one thing at a time and you will be blue to close the deal on at least one product.

After the buying

After the buying is done, if you haven't won their trust, then you won't see them again at all. They are impeccably restless and disinterested in coming back to the same place over and over again. So it is that much more important for you to pay keen attention to the people if you wish to retain them. They will buy from you whatever you offer them the next time they come in. So make sure you keep in touch with them and keep telling them about the offers that you have for them. They will be happy to hear them and come back to look at it.

When they plan to use it

These customers will be very excited to shop and have a lot of enthusiasm. So when they are using the product, if you offer to send over personnel to help them then they will be very excited about it. You can also call them and offer something new, which will further excite them. If you tell them that there is something much more useful on offer at your store then they will come running for it. They will be interested in an upgrade on what they have but expect a good deal out of it.

After using it

After they are done using the products, you have to keep them interested. You have to show them nicer and better products that will work out better for their needs. You have to lure them into coming back to you and showcase fresher products. They will love to experiment now and you can literally test out products and services on them. Even if you have one such customer, you can offer them unique offers and get them to buy them from you. Avoid showing them just one thing over and over again as it will bore them and they will look for variety. So be prepared with several parallel products and demonstrations

ready and show them different things one
after the other.

Much later

To be honest, these customers are not
interested in being loyal and will run to
another place if it catches their fancy. So you
have to put in a lot of effort to please them
and return to you. This will only be possible if
you show them variety and get them to like
whatever you have on offer. If at any point
they do lose interest, then you have to call
them up and offer something that is better
than what any other store can offer. It is
worth keeping these types of customers as
they will keep coming back for more and you
can sell them many types of products and
services.

20 – 30% customers

This category of customers will be slightly
organized but extremely confused. They will
know what to buy but will not be able to
make a choice for themselves. They will know
they need to buy biscuits but won't know
what brand. They will also be slightly obese
and walk around slowly. The best way to
influence these is to assist them in their

shopping. Volunteer to hold their shopping bag or cart and help them pick up products. By the power of suggestion you can influence them to buy things that are good for them. They will love free gifts and if you offer them complimentary products then they will be very happy. It is also a good idea to tell them that the product that they are buying is in good demand and that several people bought it on that very day.

These people are also very emotional and will settle for offers that will give them two similar products. This is because they will want to give to their loved ones gifts that can be useful to them. They will be keen on gifting to family and friends and so, you can close a sale by offering them combo offers and free gifts. The idea is to appeal to their emotional side and make use of their tendency to buy things in bulk for themselves and also for others.

During the buying process
During the buying process, you have to speak to these customers about their families and close ones. You have to empathize with their views and tell them how you are keen on helping them find things that will give them

and their loved ones useful things. Again, don't rush into it and win their trust by carrying their basket and telling them about the products and services on offer. They will be happy to be assisted and keen on taking your advice. Take them to the offers section and explain any buy 1 get 1 offer that is running in the store. You have to get them to come back to you the next time as well.

After the buying

Here too, you have to make use of the same trick. You have to give them something that will allow them to keep some and gift the rest. You can show them complimentary products but make sure that those come with some offers as well. They will happily take it and you can convert them into repeat customers. They will, however, not be interested in things that are out of their budget. Even if it is coming with a freebie, they will not buy it. They will want something that lies within their budget and is a good deal for themselves and others that they are buying for as well.

When they plan to use it

When they are using it, you can call them up and offer something that is useful with their purchase. Say for example they bought a washing machine. You can call them up and tell them about a new detergent that has the buy 1 get 1 offer running and the particular brand is great for the machine they bought. They are sure to come running to avail the offer and even better would be to get someone to take the product to them. Similarly, offer them things that will not only compliment what they have but also give them something extra.

While using it

When they are using the products, you can offer to show them demonstrations. This will help them use the products better. You can send over some people and help set it for them. They might not be able to lift some of the products and it is best that you send with them a few personal, who will help them get set up.

Much later

You can call them at any time later and offer them something interesting. Again, you can offer them and their near and dear ones something. They will be happy to take your offer and turn onto your loyal customers.

0% customers

These customers should best be ignored. They are not the type that you must care for and can ignore them. They will be present at your store only to pass time and won't be interested in buying anything. They will act like they have information on everything that there is to know about your products and that they can find better ones elsewhere. There is no point in analyzing these people at all and it is best to ignore them. If they buy something from you, then well and good, if not, forget them. But make sure you are not rude to them lest they create a ruckus and cause other customers in your shop to leave. Be obliging and allow them to do their shopping and don't bother if they walk out empty handed.

These form the various types of customers who will walk into your store and how you can retain each type.

Chapter 4: General Mistakes To Avoid

By now, I am sure you have understood the importance of having a good sales strategy and now, we will look at mistakes that you need to avoid, in general, while making a sales pitch.

Everything for everybody

There is a general misconception that it is possible for you to sell any product or service to anyone. But like I said, this is a misconception. It is not possible for you to sell anything to anyone unless they are interested in buying it. Say for example: you cannot sell a woman a shaver unless she wants it for her husband. Similarly, you have to understand what the customer wants in order for you to close a sale. By selling the right product to the right person, not only will you save on time and effort but also energy. You can focus on other things by saving time. In fact, you will see lesser returns and more repeat customers if you sell the right thing to the right person. Most shops will employ people who will keenly observe the customers who walk in and make sure they note down their likes and dislikes. They will then go to them and sell them things that they will definitely like and buy. This will ensure that the customers remain happy for long.

Talking too much

Nobody likes a person who talks too much. If you are a salesman and end up talking too much then you will only lose your customer. They will prefer to go to a store where they can peacefully shop. You must know when to stop and as soon as you have made your point, you must leave the customer. They will think about whatever you said and will act upon it if they are convinced, if not; there is nothing you can do about it. So don't go on about something and learn to give it a rest. If you see the customer walking away then make one final attempt by saying something interesting. If they come to you then it's a win for you but if they don't, then don't sweat it and focus on the next customer. There is no need to panic every time a customer walks away. Customers will come and go and there is no point in trying to talk to them incessantly. It will only cause you problems.

No aggression

Remember to never use an aggressive tone while making a pitch. Chances are you will scare away your customer. You need to maintain a high pitch when you wish to excite your customer and can maintain a low pitch when you are talking to them in general. Don't fall over them to sell a product or a service as you might come across as desperate. There will be some sales men who will use their aggressive tone and gestures to come across as dominating, this need to be avoided at all costs as it will only scare away the customers. The more love and care that you show to your customer, the better the chances of them buying from you and being your repeat customer. So speak empathetically to them and share their opinion instead of trying to prove them wrong. Many times, the customers will themselves raise their voice and try to prove the sales man wrong. In such a situation it is best to allow them to speak instead of trying to push against their voice.

Freedom to salespersons

Many companies fail to give their sales persons freedom. This means that they will instruct to say certain things and expect them to follow the same. This can make the salesperson feel bored and might not put in efforts to excite the customer. But if the sales person is given the freedom to do a little extra and express themselves in a better way then it will only profit the company. Most sales persons know the product and services better than what any of the brochures and pamphlets will provide. So it is important for the company to give the sales person's certain freedom and get them to do the talking. Although giving away too many liberties is never advisable, it is a good option to give them the freedom to express themselves to the clients in a proper way and give away their point of view on a certain product to experience better sales.

Never judge

It is best to reserve all your judgments about the customer, as you never know what their buying capacities can be. So don't judge them based on their looks, their dressing style or their accent. You must remain neutral and not pass any comments or judgments. You will be surprised at how much business someone might bring in regardless of how they appear. Remember that most big buyers will not look the part. They will look extremely standard and their sense of dressing will be quite bad. But they will splurge money and so, you must not judge them at all. There is the story of how a millionaire CEO decided to walk in dressed casually and when one store decided not to sell him anything, he ended up buying out the store in front of it. So, you never know who might be a millionaire looking to bring you a huge profit and it is best to not judge anyone.

Focus on product

Many companies and sales persons focus more on the product as opposed to the customer. This is wrong, as the primary focus, in sales, should be on the customer and not the product. You must concentrate on what the customer is saying and then pick a suitable product instead of choosing a product and looking for a suitable customer. As was mentioned before, it is important to see why the product is good for the customer and not what the product is about. You must be prepared before hand with all the features of the product and then present them in such a way that the customer takes and instant liking to it. However, don't leave out the product in the process and make sure you balance everything out.

Failing to be ready

Some people like to leave things for the last minute and when the potential customer walks in, have no response to give. This can be extremely bad for your business and so, it is important to remain ready and have everything in place before the customer, or client, walks in. The best thing to do is prepare for it the previous day. That way, you remain prepared for any type of client regardless of their mindset. You will also have the chance to answer more queries and present to them a clear idea of what your company is all about and what the product stands for. Many sales men decide to prepare just before the sale. This is the wrong move to make as not only will you be under prepared for it but also not know what to say when asked something. So it is best to prepare for it in advance and have certain answers ready so that the deal can be closed before the customer has the chance to think over it.

Over friendly

Never come across as being over friendly. It is a big turn off and you will end up chasing away your customers. This is especially a problem if you are a young man and are trying to be over friendly with a young woman. She will run out of your store and never return! Understand that the customer needs to be treated with utmost respect and appreciation. They are not there to be your friend but to buy something from you. So keep your friendliness to a minimum and don't try to come across as an over friendly person. If you think you are making the customer uncomfortable then move from there and get some one else to assist them. This will ensure that the customer is satisfied and you don't feel bad about having lost a valuable customer.

Don't stalk

One mistake that companies commit is stalking their customers. It is always advisable to keep in touch with them after a sale in order to retain them but stalking them and looking at their every move can drive them crazy. Don't bombard the same customer with several mails and messages regarding offers and deals, as it will drive them away. Have a limit to the number of mails that you send the customers. It is best to send just 2 mails per week and can be more depending on the number of customers that you have and the products that are on offer. Don't be tempted to send more when there already many customers and reserve it as an option to use when the number of customers has gone down.

Don't copy

Never copy your competitor's strategies. Do whatever works best for you and not blindly copy something that is causing them to have lots of sales. If you copy, then your customers might think of you as trying too hard, and abandon you for the other company. Be unique and try to have your own ideas. It pays to study your customer's likes and wants and then come up with unique sales and marketing strategies. In a future chapter we will read on the various marketing strategies that can be adopted and you can choose the type that best suits your company.

These form the various mistakes that you need to avoid if you wish your products and services to sell in the market. But this is not an exhaustive list and you must adopt preventive measures against the others.

Target specific selling

It is no secret that research is everything in the sales market. For this, you have to understand your target audience and do research on it. In this chapter, we will look at the various steps you need to adopt in order to sell to a particular target.

These are basic steps that any sales person will have to employ in order to expand his or her customer base. It is extremely crucial that the customer be satisfied with the product in order for them to return for it. Without this satisfaction, the customer will not come back and the sales person will have to start from scratch.

So to avoid this situation and garner a large audience base that keeps coming back for more, the sales person will have to follow 7 main steps. These steps are an indispensable part of sales strategies and you have to follow them in order in order to make positive progress.

Understanding product/ service

The very first thing for the sakes person to do is to understand the product or service thoroughly. Most sales people don't understand whether the product will be of any real use to the final customer and go on about its benefits and features. This will not make any sense to the end user, who will be keen on knowing what the product can actually do for them. So they will actually decide to walk away and not listen to what you have to say. So, do your homework on the product before you decide to find an audience for it.

Looking out

The very first thing to do is to look out for a target audience. A sale person is required to constantly look for audiences that he thinks will be interested in his products. So it is important to be on the constant look out for a customer base. He will use many techniques to serve this purpose and also look for newer techniques to be employed for the same purpose. It is a constant process and requires complete attention to attain positive results.

Contacting them

Once the target audience has been identified, it is important for the sales man to contact them for further dialogue. So he or she has to contact them and speak with them. The right approach is to get them to come to you as opposed to the other way round. If you go to them uninvited then they will turn you away but if you get them to come over to you then you have a better chance at speaking with them. If you wish to propagate the message to several people at once then you must have pamphlets and flyers printed and distributed calling people to attend a seminar that will explain the product or service to them in detail.

Need evaluation

Now before these people decide to attend your seminar, you must assess their needs. So you have to understand their expectations and what they want out of your product. Here, more than the value, you have to understand what might be bothering the customer. It is always important to show them that you have the capacity to solve their problems no matter how big they are. So your

USP is to provide them with a product or service that does not come with the problems that they are already facing from a previous brand. You are telling them that you will offer something that is unique to you and they will not experience any problems with it. This will be a lucrative prospect for them as they will be satisfied knowing you are ready to help them out no matter what the situation. So being prepared before the presentation will go a long way in helping you do the needful for your products and for your clients as well.

Presentation

The next step is to prepare a presentation for them. This is probably the most important aspect of the entire process. When it comes to the presentation, right from knowing who will partake in it to understanding as to who will help prepare the presentation is important. It is vital to understand your business first and then work as one to attract customers.

Before the presentation takes place, it is best to have one person leading the charge. This will ensure that every thing is well organized and it will be smooth sailing for all. This head or the man in charge will take all the important decisions and help you formulate a presentation that is to every body's expectations.

The ideal presentation will require you to be interactive with your audience and ask and know from them. It will be useless to go on about your own company and you will have to encourage people to speak up about their needs and wants. So get them speaking about what is bothering them with their previous products and then tell them how the problem will not arise when they use your products. This is a sure shot way to get them glued to your presentation.

Attaining results

When it comes to employing sales presentations, or any sales related steps for that matter, it is important to get the client to respond to you. This response can come in at any stage of the presentation or even before that. So right from getting these customers to say yes and attend your meeting to getting them to liking your products and presentation, the main aim at any point in time should be to solicit a positive response. Of course this is easier said than done and you will have to pay attention to whatever you are presenting to these people.

There will be those who will settle for any response that they get from these people whether it is a yes or a no. But that will do no good for you and it should be your primary focus to get people to say yes to you.

During the course of your presentation, don't cut short any of the attendees. They should feel free to speak out their mind and you must opine with them. You have to say yes to them, even if you know they are wrong. Then you must say how you have dealt with other customers who have had the same issue and cite appropriate examples to win their confidence. Doing so will impress them and get them to say yes to whatever you ask or tell them.

Chapter 5: Ideal Sales Person Qualities

A salesman should possess certain qualities that will make him ideal to sell to a variety of people. The sales man has to deal with a hoard of people on a daily basis and it becomes increasingly difficult for him to maintain his calm composure. So to be alert and active in every situation, he must develop both a mental and a physical stamina along with certain virtues that will help him turn into the most ideal sales man.

In this chapter, we will look at the qualities of an ideal salesman in detail.

Open minded

The very first quality to possess is open mindedness. Sales men need to interact with a lot of people and they will have to put up with all types of mindsets. Being open minded cannot only make it easier to speak with the people but also drive across a point. So it is vital for the person to be as open minded as possible. There can be those who will not think freely and go into a meeting or presentation with a closed mindset. Such salesmen will not be able to even close a single sale. So it is important to be as open minded as possible if you wish to be a successful sales man.

Focused

It is important for a sales man to maintain focus on a variety of things. This includes the client; the product pitch etc. if the sales man's focus deviates then he or she will not be able to close a deal well enough. No customer wants a sales man who is not paying attention to them and is constantly looking around. So you, as a sales man, must maintain constant focus and come up with a technique that will help you from losing focus. It can be a physical movement like the snapping of fingers to help you re focus.

Innovative

It is extremely important for the sales man to be innovative. Innovation is vital for all creative people. Depending on the situation, he or she must come up with an innovative idea to rescue a bad presentation or sale deal. It will require fast thinking and coming up with an idea that is both practical and meaningful. This type of trait can only be developed over a period of time and will not come by easily. Practice is key and the more you do it, the more profound its gets.

Expressive

Being expressive is a great quality for a sales man to have. How he or she behaves with the client is important. Right from speaking the right words to making hand and body gestures, being expressive is a great way to trap the client's attention. They will be drawn to how you act and want to see what you are telling others. They will also be interested in hearing what you are saying and ideally reply in the affirmative to your sales queries. So it is important to be as expressive as possible to be a good sales man.

Responsible

As a sales man representing an entire company, it is important to be as responsible as possible. The weight that sales men carry on their shoulders is generally quite heavy but that should not affect their responsibility. They must be determined to take on any challenge head on and find a solution to the problem. If something needs to be done then he or she must spring into action and make sure that it gets done. Communication is vital and the sales man must communicate with his team members and also clients and make sure that everything is completed responsibly by the end of the day.

Observance

Having keen observation is another important quality for a salesman to have. He or she should observe the latest trends, choices, fashions etc. This will tell them about the current tastes and preferences of the people. Observing keenly is always important even in the busiest of situations. A good sales man will not forget what he had observed and use it to his advantage at a later time.

Empathetic

Empathy relates to understanding a problem or situation from the point of view of the customer. He or she must understand their problems and empathize with them instead of talking back to them. The more the empathy; the better the sales, so it is important to empathize with the client and look at things through their point of view to close a sale!

Resourceful

Resourcefulness is another trait that a good sales man must possess. The sales man must think of alternatives as soon as possible and use them to handle a situation. This will require quick thinking and the sales man will have to come up with alternate solutions to issues as soon as possible.

Active

A good sales man will be active and energetic. He will not say "no" to anything and be ready to take up any challenge. It is important to be of sound health and have the capacity to land anywhere at a moment's notice. This is not possible fi the person is lazy and generally disinterested. He or she must get up and run if required to help a customer or showcase a product or service.

Pleasant looks

A sales man must be well kept. Right from hair to clothes, everything must be tiptop. Pleasant looks are important for not just the onlookers sake but for personal reasons as well. A well-groomed sales man will be extremely confident and better equipped at closing a sale.

These form the various traits that a good sales man must possess.

Chapter 6: Training Salesmen

It is important to train your sales men from time to time. They will have to be trained in the different departments, as they will be representing your company to the public. So it is up to you to train them and provide them with the best in the business.

In this chapter, we will look at the various training techniques you can adopt to train your sales men.

E training

E training refers to electronic training. In this method, you provide your staff with videos and links to training videos, which they can watch and learn from. This is a great technique to adopt as they can study from anywhere and at any time. You can also save on a lot of costs by adopting this technique. You can get an expert trainer to upload videos for you. You can also put in videos describing the product or service so that they can remain well informed about it and use it to their advantage. You can provide them with a small tablet each, which can play the videos for them.

Reward training

Reward training refers to setting challenges for your dales men and training them in the process. The one who successfully understands and executes the tasks will be rewarded for his or her good work. Many organizations prefer to keep it a secret and check whether their sales men are up to the mark. But you can announce it and get them to work hard to avail the reward. The reward must be lucrative enough for them and they should think of it as a bonus and work hard to earn it.

Field training

Field training is an age-old type of training technique. Here, the company provides on field training to their employees. They will place them in their natural environment and provide them with appropriate training. Field training is an important part of any organization and it is best to incorporate it even if you are using any of the other forms of training as well. Here too, you can announce reward for the best sales men and keep their morale high.

Role playing

Role-playing refers to a few sales men acting as the customers and some as the sales man. This will give them a hands on experience and train them to do their best in any situation. You can employ this technique on a monthly basis, and get them to pose as different groups of customers. Make sure there is a rotation in the roles and the same ones are not made the customers or the sales men. Once you get them to act it out, they will know exactly how to interact with real customers and you can experience bigger and better sales.

Example training

Example training refers to telling sales men about case studies and giving them examples about other sales men. They will understand things better if you give them appropriate examples and tell them about certain situations that might arise at the work place. These examples are best demonstrated and the sales men will get a clearer picture from it.

Senior training

This is better known as a one to one training. Each sales man is paired up with a senior, who has worked as a sales man for many years. He or she will be able to pass on their experience and also introduce the sales men to certain techniques that they used. You can get qualified seniors to help you out with the job!

These are just some of the methods that you can adopt but it is not limited to these. Remember that there are many other such techniques that you can adopt and train your sales men. It is important to pay individual attention to each sales man and not club them into large groups. The time taken by each one to learn these techniques will also differ and it is best to give everyone ample time to understand something. Don't rush anybody into anything and make sure every body is happy to participate in the training process.

Chapter 7: Market Research

Market research is an important part of any company and it is vital to perform timely research. Right from big companies to small ones, everybody conducts market research and it is considered to be a vital part of any company's sales strategy. Its meaning, importance and steps are discussed in detail in this chapter.

Meaning

As the name suggests, market research refers to conducting research for your product in the market. It is important to conduct this research and garner information on a variety of topics. These include understanding the target market, analyzing the reach of the product, understanding people's perception etc. All these need to be understood in order for a product or a service to sell better.

Importance

There are many benefits to conducting market research and they are mentioned as under.

Understanding current customers

By conducting market research, you can thoroughly understand the wants and needs of your current customers. You have the chance to get an insight into their psyche and know what they like and dislike about your products or services. You will know why they choose certain products from your brand and the rest from a competitor's brand. What factors are influencing them to settle for a product from your company? Where are they hearing about your product and what is drawing them to it? What is the demographic and why are they interested in the products that they are buying from you. All these questions will be answered and you will have the chance to reach to more customers.

Understanding new audience

Apart from understanding the existing customers, market research will help you identify potential customers as well. You will have the chance to identify newer customers and why they are likely to buy your products. You can know their wants and needs and make custom made products for them. You can also know their age, their gender, likes and dislikes and have a thorough insight on your customer base. Many companies, new and old, splurge on this one process and ensure that their products and services reach a wide audience.

Apart from these there are many other benefits that a company can avail by conducting market research such as solving any issues in the company, improving their marketing strategy, coming up with a new line of products, increasing the communication with the audience, evaluating the progress of the company etc. All these are important for a company to consider and taking care of these will ensure that you crush your sales numbers!

Steps involved in market research

Market research, in reality, is an elaborate process. There are many things to do and it is important for you to follow a standard step-by-step procedure for it. In this segment, we look at the different steps you must adopt to conduct market research.

Step 1 Understanding the problem

The very first step to adopt in market research is to identify the problem that the company is facing. There will be an inherent problem that the company will face and it will be up to the research team to analyze and understand the problem. The issue might not be present at just one level and it might exist at several levels. It is up to the team to find out what the problem at each level is and then tackle each at a time.

Step 2 Setting objectives
The second step is to formulate objectives for the research. This involves preparing questionnaires, preparing hypothesis, understanding a mode of distribution and survey etc. The main objective is to be prepared for the market research and make sure the process is well though for. It will be a herculean task to perform it and the researcher needs to be ready for anything that might come his way while conducting the research.

Step 3 planning and designing
You have to plan the market research in order to carry it out smoothly. For this, you must understand the various factors that affect it. You will need to plan out a mode of conduct as well and take measures to put it into action. The designing part involves formulating a step-by-step process to be

adopted for the research. The researcher must try to understand the various sources that will be tested for the research and establish a link with them.

Step 4 Sampling

The next step is known as sampling. Sampling is a procedure where the researcher chooses a small population to test out. This helps him understand how the larger population is thinking. A sample is always seen as a small concentrated group that will provide relevant information meant to help researchers understand the over all market mood. For this, he should determine the size of the population and know how many people will be included in it. It is important for the group to contain individual elements of all the different categories of people that will be part of the research audience.

Step 5 Collecting data

Collecting data refers to collecting relevant information, which will be used to solve the problem effectively. It is meant to be a set of data that is used to arrive at market research conclusions. This data collection is a vital part of the process and something that ties everything together. The researcher will distribute all the questionnaires to the people and get them to answer certain questions, which will give them an idea about the different mindsets that are present in the market.

Step 6 Analyzing

The next logical step for the researcher to adopt is analyzing the data collected. For this, he or she will collect all the data that is available and go through it and understand it. They will then simplify the data to be used and further researched. If the data collected is sufficient then they will try to arrive at conclusions based on it but if they feel like its insufficient then they will decide to conduct further research on the topic. Most researchers use both analytical and statistical tools to analyze data and use it to formulate solutions to issues in regard to their products and services.

Step 7 Conclusions

The last step is to prepare solutions and conclusions for the market research. By now, they would have collected all the relevant information from the market and have a clear picture of what is happening with the product in the market. They will then come up with solutions for the business, which when implemented, will help them see positive results and growth. The researcher is given the chance to have his or her say in the matter and personally suggest something that will be of use to the company and help them better their sales in the future.

Market research is important for any company and it is best for all companies to take it up and use it to avail greater sales. These are the general steps that need to be followed but it is up to you to tweak these and come up with additional steps to suit your business model. Don't copy something that your competitor is doing as each and every business has a unique identity and you have to formulate your own strategy to make positive progress.

Chapter 8: Marketing Techniques

There are many marketing techniques out there and you have to choose the type that fits your needs. In this chapter, we will look at the different marketing techniques that you can adopt for your company.

Relationship marketing

Relationship marketing is the best type of marketing to choose for your brand. As the name suggests, relationship marketing refers to building a relationship with the customers and not merely selling them your products. If a customer falls in love with your brand, then chances are he or she will buy more and more from you. So it is important to establish a strong relationship with your customers and get them to like you and your marketing stretches. As per market survey, a customer is likely to buy from you 6 times more if he or she loves your brand.

Proximity marketing

Proximity marketing refers to selling products and services to those that lie close to your place. Although modern day meaning refers to sending marketing messages to people's phones and tablets that lie close to you, it also signifies selling these to those that lie close to you. Proximity marketing will help you save on a lot of money and you get to sell more to people. It is not tough to carry out such marketing and you will only need a few messages and messengers to give out the message to the customers that lie around you.

Transactional marketing

Transactional marketing refers to luring people into your store by running offers and discounts. This will ensure that you lure many customers into your store and get them to buy from you. Most big retailers depend on this trick and you can capitalize on it as well. It will not be difficult to come up with sales and discount strategies and all you will need is a team of marketers who will formulate these strategies for you. With time, you will know what to offer to your customers and experience great sales.

Call to action marketing

Call to action marketing refers to telling people to buy your product. This is possible if you have a strong online presence and can reach out to a lot of people. You can put links to your website and get people to click on it and buy your products. They will find it easier to place an order online as opposed to visiting your store for it. You will be able to get a lot of people on your website and even if 3/4ths buy your product then it will be a lucrative offer for you.

Viral marketing

Viral marketing, as the name suggests, refers to your marketing strategies going viral. You will post an ad in a social media platform and many people will like it and share it. News about the product will start to spread and in no time, you will have a sea of customers all want I g your product. But the problem with this type is, it is possible for people to drag down your product. There will be competitors who will purposely tag you and show you in bad light. This can be quite hampering for your brand's image. So it is important to control who gets to tag you where and who gets to comment on your offers.

Scarcity marketing

Scarcity marketing refers to controlling the amount of product that is released n the market. This is a great marketing stretchy that can be adopted by both small and big companies. When a product is released in the market and there are many takers for it, the demand for the product will shoot up. At such a time, if the product is not supplied then people will want it that much more. When the product is released again, in limited supply then amazing sales are sure to come by. This is a great technique to use for all those interested in experiencing high sales.

Mass marketing

Mass marketing reefs to catering to the masses. This is seen as the most expensive form of marketing as you are required to focus on each and every segment of the market and design appropriate strategies for each. This will ensure that the right product reaches the right customer. This is ideal for big coma lines that have a large finance and are capable of reaching out to the masses. It is best if the company has many branches spread all over the country, as it will work out to be cost effective.

Undercover marketing

Under cover marketing refers to teasing the audience and not giving them the whole picture. This can generate a lot of curiosity amongst them and make them extremely enthusiastic. They will then want to know more about your product and put in efforts to find out about it. This strategy will work great with youth who will be enthusiastic to know about the new products in the market. You must place these teasers in places where the audience can easily find them. This can be on billboards, in social media and also television if you can afford it.

Diversity marketing

Diversity marketing refers to coming up with unique marketing techniques that can be applied to a diverse group of people. As you know, there will be different types of people in the market all separated by religion, beliefs, gender, tastes, wants etc. if you have the resources to cater to all of these then you can perform diversity marketing. It will cost you qui a bit but it will be well worth the effort, as you will have an opportunity to create tailor made marketing strategies.

Online marketing/ Email marketing

Online marketing refers to using the online platform to create brand and product awareness. It is possible for you to promote your brand and products by choosing online resources such as social media platforms, pop up ads, blogs and also emails. It is possible to reach out to a wide audience by making use of these. You can send custom mails to people and get them to like your products. They will be drawn to your special offs as well. If you can tie up with a store like eBay or amazon, then you can sell your products there too! All you have to do is create a page for yourself and enlist all your products. You can mention it on blogs or on your website. Many times, those online stores will give away attractive offers and discounts without affecting your profit margin. That will ensure better sales for you. The Internet is a great tool to use for marketing and if you don't, then you will be left behind.

Seasonal marketing

Seasonal marketing refers to designing products and services that are season specific. This will ensure that you have a product that is carrying the season's flavor. For example, you can change the graphics of your product and incorporate a seasonal element like snow or a snowman. This will appeal to the audience and they will be interested in buying it as a souvenir. It pays to change it up from season to season as people can easily get bored of something if they don't see any variety in it.

Evangelistic marketing

Evangelistic marketing refers to identifying those special customers that are true blue fans of your company. These people can be made representatives of your brand and they will be more than happy to promote you. They will literally go out of their way to promote your brand and help you find new customers. You can also decide to pay them a certain fee if you like and get them to promote your brand in a bigger and better way.

Event marketing

Event marketing refers to coming up with events that go along with the sales and discounts. That way, you will have more people visiting your store and busing your products. You can hold a small event or a big one depending on your budget. The event will not only be the center of attraction but also help you find a lot of new customers. It is best to have these events timed with festivals and other holidays as you can expect a lot of people to visit.

Inbound marketing

In bound marketing refers to selling products and services to people who are already customers. There will be a lot of customers calling in to find out about something and it will be a great opportunity to sell them other products and services that will be on offer at your place. So not only are they themselves calling you, they are also most likely to say yes to whatever you plan to put in offer for them.

Outbound marketing

This is the opposite of inbound marketing. Here, the companies will get new customers to calm in and try to sell them products and services. These would have called based on a tip that they would have gotten from existing customers. So this can be capitalized upon and it will be a great opportunity for the company to find new customers for their company.

Newsletter marketing

This is a very traditional method and still remains to be the most popular. In this method, you send out newsletters to your customers mentioning the offers and discounts that you will be announcing soon. They will read your offers and come by to avail it. Similarly, you can also reach out to a bigger audience and send out newsletters to a lot more people. Apart from the firs and discounts you can also mention any news items and changes that have happened in your company. All these will appeal to the and audience and such interactivity will help you increase your communication with your customers.

Freebie marketing

Freebie marketing refers to giving away free things with the products and services you have on offer. You can give away anything that you like but make sure it is related to the main product in question. Most people prefer to give away something that is of a complimentary or supplementary nature to the main product. It will only help the company sell more and also find a larger audience base.

Niche marketing

Niche marketing refers to specific target products that are promoted in the market. These products are made specifically for a particular segment of the market, which the manufacturer feels will definitely consume it. For example, a particular lipstick range is aimed at young girls, who are looking for beauty and benefits from it. So they will design ad campaigns centering around the lipstick and launch it in colleges.

Drip marketing

Drip marketing refers to sending out messages to the media about a product so that they propagate the message to the audience. This will ensure that the ad reaches a wider audience and the product is availed by many people. It is a strategy that most big retailers adopt and is considered one of the best ones to take up for any company.

These form the different marketing strategies that you can adopt and improve your sales numbers.

Chapter 9: Sales Strategy Models

When it comes to sales strategies, there are a few important models that have been formulated over the years. These models are based on several market factors that aid in the sales process. So it is a matter of brining all the relevant data together and using it to avail higher sales. In this chapter, we will look at these models in detail and tell you about its true meaning and uses.

3 C Model

The first model that we will look at is known as the 3c model. The 3 c model is a strategic model that aims at helping companies increase their sales within a short period of time. The 3 c's that are involved here include the customers, the competitors and the corporation. These are the 3 c's that the company must keep happy in order for them to operate optimally and avail better sales. As you know, the customers are the most important part of the sales strategy. The company needs to keep them as happy as possible in order to get them buying more and more of their products and services. If a company fails to keep their customers happy, then it will be impossible for them to survive. When it comes to availing success, a company will always keep an eye on their competitors. The company will have to analyze their strategies and come up with some that are better. Only then can they capture a market share greater than their rival's. The corporation stands for the company itself. If the company itself is struggling and there are internal problems and bickering, then it will not work well for them. So, they must first solve the problems that lie internally and then look outwardly to increase their sales. Apart from these, there are also 3 other c's, being capability, consistency and cultivation, which will also help the company see better sales.

4P model

Just like the 3c model, there is another one known as the 4 p model. The 4 p model includes product, price, promotion and place. These are the elements that guide a sales strategy and it is important for the company to look into each one and improve upon to see positive results. As you know, product refers to the product that is sold in the market. This product is the star of the show and so; it is vital for the company to pay keen attention to it. The price also plays an important role in the success of a product. It will determine whether people will buy it or think it is too high. So the company needs to do some careful thinking in order to set an appropriate price for the product and get more and more people to buy it. The next P stands for promotion. Promoting a product is of extreme importance. Without proper promotions, people will not be able to know of the uses and importance of buying the particular product. So, the company has to put in some extra efforts to promote the product and make sure it reaches the right audience. The last P stands for place. Place refers to the marketing channel for the products. The channel is important as the goods should reach the people in a short amount of time and it should be cost effective for the company. These form the 4 main P's that are involved in the sales strategy of the business and it is important for any company to pay keen attention to it. Apart from these, there are also 3 extra P's that stand for people, process and physical evidence. People, as we know, relates to the customers that are one of the most important aspects of the business. Process refers to the process that is adopted to market the business. Physical evidence refers to the delivery of the product or service and people's feedback on it. All these will account for a company's success or failure in regard to their sales strategies. A company must focus on all 7 p's and make sure that all of them are working together for them.

Customer lifetime value model

Customer lifetime value model is a model that is used to check the over all value that a customer will derive out of the products and services that the company puts on offer. This is used to understand the true value of the products and services that are on offer for people to consume. It will help the company estimate the cash flows from the products that are consumed by the customers. This cash flow analysis is important to understand how the company will fare and what they will have in the future. Future planning is of vital importance for most companies and it is best for them to make use of this particular model to get the exact picture. Most companies use this strategy to check how their sales strategies are faring. It will be encouraging for them to take up sales strategies that are good for the lifetime of the company and are not merely meant to help them see temporary results. This strategy will also help them find appropriate customers for themselves and aim their products at the right groups. It is easy for any company to adopt these strategies and it will benefit them in the long run.

All of these are together known as marketing mix and each company will have their own mix to use. It is important that this mix is a combination of all of these models and together, they help the company experience bigger and better sales. Most companies will employ experts, who will help them formulate the best marketing mix strategies to help their company avail better sales.

Chapter 10: Internal Analysis Of A Business

When it comes to formulating an effective sales strategy, it is important for the company to analyze both its internal and external environments. In this chapter, we will look at the two types of analysis that will help the company come up with sales strategies aimed at increasing their overall potential.

Swot analysis

Swot stands for strengths weakness opportunities and threats. These are the main points where the company has to focus and analyze its internal situation. Let us look at each of these in detail.

Strengths

Strengths of a company refer to the various strengths that the company possesses. These strengths are what help the company capture a market share. In order to understand the true strength of the company, there are a few basic, yet important, questions that need to be answered and they are as follows.

Where is our sales strategy going right?

This is an important question to ask and answer. It will tell you where your strategy is going right and where it is not. Once you successfully answer this question, you will know exactly where your strength lies. You have to collect data about your strategy and look at where it is working well for you. It will help you to consult the team that is responsible for the formulation of the strategy.

How does the public perceive it?

This is the next important question to answer. It will tell you how others perceive your sales strategies. It is important to understand this bit and look at things from an outsider's perspective. You will have the chance to know whether or not your message is coming across as you intend it to.

What is your USP?

Each and every company needs to have a unique selling proposition. You have to understand yours and whether it can be bettered. Once you have the answer to it, you will understand how important it is for you to have a unique USP. If you think it can be bettered, then you must put in efforts to do so.

These form the various strength related questions that you need to ask and answer to improve your sales strategy.

Weakness

Weakness refers to the weaknesses that your company has. This weakness is nothing to be scared of and is an opportunity for you to better your sales strategy. Here are a few questions you need to answer to understand this topic better.

What are your sales weaknesses?
It is obvious that a company will not always only have strengths. They will also have weaknesses, which have to be dealt with. In order to do so, you must ask this vital question and have it answered. Look at the problems that exist in your sales strategy and see if they can be remedied.

What factors are causing the flaws?

The next question to ask and answer is what could be causing the flaws in your sales strategy? It could be a combination of factors and you have to understand each one to know what could be contributing towards it.

What is the market's perception of your weaknesses?

The market will have a view on your weaknesses and you must understand it to know it from an outsider's point of view. Once you come to know, you can work on them to improve your sales strategy.

Opportunities

Opportunities, as you know, refer to the opportunities that are available to you to exploit. Here are some questions on the topic that we need to look at to understand the topic better.

What are good opportunities to exploit?

What are some of the good opportunities out there that you can exploit and use to your advantage? Is it possible for you to incorporate newer challenges and use them to your advantage?

What are the current trends doing the rounds?

It is important to understand the current trends that are doing the rounds in the market. You will have a fair idea of all the things that you can possibly do to improve your sales potential.

What are people's suggestions?

Here too, you must take the advice of an outsider. So look at what people, including your customers are telling you to do and make sure you incorporate them into your business.

Threats

Threats, as you know, refer to the threats that are present inside and outside your company. These threats are what will ultimately bring you down, if you don't keep a tab on them. Here are a few questions and answers that you need to look at in this regard.

What are you hurdles?

The first question to ask and answer is what are the hurdles that lie on the way for you?

Are they within your organization or outside of it? Is there something that is preventing your sales strategy from becoming a success? These are important questions that you must ask and answer.

What is your competition up to?

It is vital to understand what your competition is up to. They will be doing something to garner a bigger audience for their products and you have to try and seek inside information on it. They will, of course, want to know your secrets too, and it is important that you try to keep it as secretive as possible.

Are your threats really bad?

You have to know whether your threats are really bad and if they are causing you to lose potential customers. If they really are that bad, then it is best to address them at the earliest possible time and not move forward without addressing it.

This SWOT analysis is extremely important for any company and it is best to perform it from time to time. The ideal time to do it is every quarterly, so that you are well informed about your company and have a good sales strategy in place.

Apart from the SWOT analysis, you can also perform the PEST or the PESTLE analysis. But that incorporates studying both the forces present inside the organization as well as outside influencers. The choice is yours and you can take up all of these if you like or just stick with one.

Chapter 11: After Sales Service

Having a good after sales services is an extremely important part of a good sales strategy. If you don't provide your customers with after sales services then they will not be satisfied with your services at all. In this chapter, we look at some of the important after sales services that you need to incorporate in your sales strategy to help increase its potential.

Availability

It is extremely important to be available for your customers at all times. Even if they wish to reach out to you late at night, you must be available to help them. They might have certain doubts about the product or the service and you have to hire people who will be available to answer their questions and give them advice. It is best to provide them with a phone number that they can dial at any time and avail information about the product. Make sure the lines are free and not always busy as that can annoy your clients.

Gratitude

Make sure you thank your customers when they buy something from you. It is important to tell them how grateful you are and why you value them. You can send them a personal thank you note or add it into their packing. It will go a long way in establishing a good relationship with your customers. Make sure you give it to every one and not miss out on any customer as they might take it offensively. So check for all the products that leave your store to make sure it is present in all.

Information

Once your customers buy products from you, you have to provide them with information to help use the products better. You can arrange for a demonstration that will help them understand how to use something and also help in setting it up for them. Once you have everything readied, you can show them how to use it on a daily basis. You can either give them instruction manuals or personally visit them.

Guarantees

Although no store gives away guarantees these days, it is important to consider the customer's value and offer them a replacement for a bad product. Many times, the customer themselves will be clumsy with a product and end up breaking it. They will then call up and say they got it broken. In such a case too, you must oblige and offer to replace the product for them. If they do it again then it is not worth entertaining them. But given your loyalty, you might and up converting bad customers into your 80-90% customers.

Offers

It is important to send offers to your customers. They must be made aware of the different offers that you have running at your store, so that they can come over and avail them. These offers should be your USP and they should be lured into buying from you. You must send them customized mails and can also send physical pamphlets and let them know about the different offers that you have running at any given point in time. It is best to send them offers on complimentary products.

Personalized service

Many times, it pays to establish a relationship with the customers. These customers are interested in being your loyal buyers and so, you must pay attention to each and every one. In this day and age where everybody has an online presence, it is best to track your customers' social media pages and know what they are up to. You can then send them personalized messages and also gifts to tell them how involved you are in their lives. They will appreciate your gesture and will be happy to be your promoters.

Special offers

Special offers are unique offers that you send to only certain customers. If you have some that regularly buy from you and create a lot of business for you, then you can offer them something unique, which you don't offer to anybody else. This will give them a unique feeling and they will be happy to receive such offers. You must specifically tell them that these offers are unique and tailored only for them and that availing these will give them a unique advantage.

Special events

You can organize special events for your special customers. Everybody wishes to feel unique and special and you can help them do so by organizing these parties. They will be made to partake in the event and mingle with other special customers. It will be a good opportunity for you to address all your loyal customers at once and make them feel special. These parties can be organized once a year and you must send out special and personal invites well in advance. You must choose a location that is convenient for a majority of the audience and arrange for food and drinks to turn it into a festivity. Such celebrations will only work to your greater advantage.

Rewards

Offering special rewards such as loyalty points are a great sales strategy to employ. You have the chance to reward your customers for their loyalty and they will be happy to avail discounts thanks to their purchases. The reward points must always be on the higher side and not measly. It is best to attach an expiry date to the points so that, you create a sense of urgency and get them to use it up before time runs out. You can send them emails that ask and persuade them to use up their points and they will feel the need to buy something from you.

Involvement

It is a great idea to involve your customers as much as possible and get them to suggest changes for you. They will give away all the best suggestions and acting upon them will help you increase your sales. You can either pass out forms to be filled or can also ask them to complete an online questionnaire. Ultimately, you will have the chance to get an outsider's opinion and improve your business based on it.

These form the various after sales services that you can adopt to improve your business.

Chapter 12: Modern Take On Sales Strategies

It is obvious that sales strategies will not remain the same over a long period of time and they will change depending on the market conditions. In this chapter, we look at some modern takes on sales strategies and why they are better choices for you as opposed to old school strategies.

Partnering

It is a good idea to partner with someone and do a joint marketing strategy. That way, you save on a lot of costs and also have the potential to improve your reach. You can partner with someone who has been in the marketing business for a long time. Many companies decide to tie up with other companies that are in the same line as them and an alliance will only bring about harmony, respect and open up an avenue of opportunities.

People's power

The Internet is now a force to reckon with. It is possible for you to use people's power to generate ad campaigns for yourself. All you have to do is create a Facebook page for yourself and get people to share their stories, humor, content etc. You can then use all of it in your business campaign and involve these customers as much as possible. His will make it appear genuine and others will love to associate with your brand. You can employ a creative person to tie it all together for you.

Blogs, websites

Just like using social media, it is also a great idea to use blogs and websites to your advantage. Look for powerful and influential bloggers capable of making you popular and reaching out to a large audience. You can get them to speak about you and mention your story in their content. Affiliate marketing comes next, where you get them to sprinkle all your product links in their blogs. Their readers will then click on your links and end up buying your products. Making use of such a marketing strategy is always a good opportunity to capitalize on the power of the Internet.

Easy problem solving

Many times, you will not have enough information on a product owing not having used it personally. In such a case, if someone comes to you with a problem, you might not be able to help them well enough. So, to help solve this problem, you can create an online community that asks certain questions about the product and get users to answer it for you. Such questions and answers page will help you see increased sales and you will find your products flying off of their shelves!

Live sessions

Just like the blogs and websites, you can host live sessions on the Internet. Better known as podcasts, you can help your customers interact with you. They will ask and have their questions answered and all you need to do is get them to tweet to you or ask a question on a social media platform. It will go a long way in helping you understand the importance of establishing a close relationship with your customers and why you must get them to interact with each other as well. When one person asks a question then others will also benefit from it.

Experiment!

Don't stick to the same strategies time and again. You must introduce as much variety as possible and get people to reach out to you. You cannot reach out to all of your customers by using just one type of platform and must put in efforts to exploit all the choices on offer and make sure you are pleasing all types of crowds. You can employ a specific person to take care of all your social media interactions and reply to all the queries that people post there.

Employee involvement

There was a time when companies relied only on experts to come up with sales strategies for them. They were given the task of coming up with effective sales strategies and nobody else was consulted for a second opinion. But now, they rely on every body's opinions as people have grown smarter and are more involved in their day-to-day operations. So it is a good idea to get your employees to suggest to you certain ideas that will help improve your sales strategies. You can pass around a questionnaire and get them to answer certain important questions, which will make it easier for you to incorporate their opinions.

Make it interesting

A standard campaign will not cut it and you must make it as interesting as possible for yourself and your customers. Make it a fun activity and not a serious and drab one. Your customers will love it if you give them a fun and interactive session to partake in. you can organize competitions and give away gifts to all the best performers. You can also organize interactive games for them, which will not only generate an interest amongst them but also get them to understand the product or service better.

Nostalgia marketing

This is a great way to recapture the customers that you once had for your products. Nostalgia marketing involves making use of old ideals that you company once used to promote their products. Using the same ideals again can help you refresh people's memories and help them fall in love with your products once again. Look at old ads that your company had put out and bring them back. Your audience will relate with it better and you can also introduce the concept to new customers.

These are just some of the modern takes on sales strategies and it is not limited to these. You can use them and increase your company's sales.

Key highlights

The very first thing to do is to understand the importance of an effective sales strategy. Sales strategies are a vital part of any business and it is important to adopt one that is effective and easy to apply. Right from small companies to big ones, everybody needs a good sales strategy to adhere to and exploit them to their maximum potential. We looked at the various important advantages of employing a good sales strategy and you can go through them again to convince yourself to take it up and employ them in your business.

One of the most important sales strategies to employ is known as the 80/20 analysis. This is a strategy that helps companies arrive at statistical numbers for their product-customer relationship. The theory states that 80% of your business will come from 20% of your customers. Also, 20% of your products will bring you 80% profits. There is a statistical method that you can employ to arrive at these statistics. You can employ someone to do the mathematical analysis for you and help you arrive at the exact numbers and know who should be your target audience and which ones are your best selling products.

There are many sales strategies that you can employ to increase your product and service sales. These strategies have been carefully formulated and are meant to act as your true sales guides. You must carefully evaluate each one and understand their true nature and value. Once you choose the best ones for yourself, you must implement them and use them to better your business. The strategies are aimed at helping you improve your sales and you must pay attention to each one if you wish to exploit it to its highest potential.

Customer retention is an important part of any business. It should be considered a part of the sales strategy to identify the different types of customers that walk in through the door and provide them with specialized services. This is important as 1 old customer is as good as 10 new ones and so, it is better to hold on to existing ones and sell to them as opposed to finding new ones. There are different categories of customers such as the

80% to 90%, the 60% to 40% etc. All these are separate categories and you must identify specific customers from your lot to cater to them individually.

There are many mistakes to avoid when it comes to employing sales strategies. These mistakes can make or break it for you and you must pay attention to them. It is up to you to understand them thoroughly and make sure that they are not part of your sales strategies. You must look into your current strategies to see if they are already in existence and then root them out at the earliest. If they are not there, then you must avoid their entry into your sales strategies and formulate some that do not incorporate them.

There are certain sales man qualities that every ideal sales man must possess. It will be difficult for a single sales man to promote an entire range of products and services and so, there should be certain virtues that he must abide by, in order to close the sale better. These are generic qualities that he must possess and will help him reach out to a bigger audience. He as to put in efforts to understand these qualities and then employ them to attain better sales results! It will take some time for him to develop these and patience will pay off positively.

A company must put in efforts to provide their sales men with appropriate training. All sales men require training and it is up to you to provide them with it. You can follow the various steps mentioned in this book and train your salesmen to perform better every time. But you must not limit yourself to just these and come up with appropriate training techniques that can be employed in your organization. Remember that not all salesmen are alike and you must provide each with a different training technique.

There are 3 types of sales strategy models that you need to learn about and use them to formulate effective sales strategies. You will realize that they are quite effective in helping you come up with guidelines that will aid in increasing your sales. You don't have to study them in detail but if you do, you will understand the differences in each and how they can collectively help you increase your sales potential.

Foolproof Method to CRUSH Your Numbers - Selling, Sales Techniques, and Sales Strategy

Market research is extremely important. You have to understand your target audience in order to know whether or not they are interested in your products and services. If they have any issues, then you must enlist help to fix the problems. If you don't address their issues then you will end up losing your customers. There are certain steps that you need to follow for your market research. It is best to follow the steps in an orderly fashion to avail the best results. It is best to employ experts to do it for you and it pays to employ the best in the business.

There are almost 100 types of marketing techniques and you must choose the ones that best suit your business. Don't choose something that is not easy to adopt and pick a technique that your company can easily put into practice. We looked at 20 of the best marketing strategies available and you can choose any one of them for your products and services. Remember, your marketing techniques are what will get your products and company noticed and you must do your best to choose the best ones for yourself.

Conducting internal research is crucial for any business. The information that you collect from there will help you come up with good sales strategies. The best strategy to conduct an internal research is known as the SWOT analysis, which helps you identify your strengths, weaknesses, opportunities and threats. You must ask and answer questions in regard to each one and you will have the chance to exploit each of these aspects. Once you have answers to all your questions, you can use the data to formulate effective strategies for your business.

After sales services are an important part of your sales strategies. You have to keep the customer happy for long, if you wish to avail consistent business from them. You can do that by being available for them even after selling them a product or a service. There are many things that you can do to provide your customers with appropriate after sales services and it is best to implement them one at a time, as rushing into all can spell disaster. Give one service time to settle in with your customers, before moving to another one.

Foolproof Method to CRUSH Your Numbers - Selling, Sales Techniques, and Sales Strategy

Modern day sales strategies are quite unique and help you keep with the times. You can implement them and attain better results. You will have the chance to appeal to older customers and newer ones as well. You must make maximum use of the Internet and social media. You must also tap into your customer's potential and use their power to reach out to a wider and diverse audience. You can increase your sales potential by doing so.

Conclusion

I thank you once again for choosing this book and hope you had a good time reading it.

Improving your sales is quite an easy job if you know what you need to do. All companies need advice on their sales strategies and having an outsider's perspective can help quite a bit.

You can conduct surveys to understand if you are doing things right and then work on your sales strategies. You must consider all the advice that is mentioned in this book, and hope you have understood them thoroughly.

The next step is for you to apply these strategies and improve your sales numbers and close all your deals with ease. I wish you luck with all your endeavors and hope you find immense success with your sales.

Best of luck!